IN THE DANGEROUS CL

IN THE DANGEROUS CLOAKROOM

KATHRYN DASZKIEWICZ

Shoestring Press

Printed by imprintdigital
Upton Pyne, Exeter
www.imprintdigital.net

Typeset by types of light
typesoflight@gmail.com

Published by Shoestring Press
19 Devonshire Avenue, Beeston, Nottingham, NG9 1BS
(0115) 925 1827
www.shoestringpress.co.uk

First published 2006. New edition 2015.

ISBN 978-1-910323-16-8

ACKNOWLEDGEMENTS

Acknowledgements are due to the editors of the following publications in which some of these poems first appeared or are due to appear: *Critical Survey, Dream Catcher, The Frogmore Papers, The Interpreter's House, Mslexia, Orbis, Other Poetry, Pennine Platform, Poetry Nottingham, Prop, The Red Wheelbarrow, The Rialto, Seam, Smiths Knoll, Staple, Tears in the Fence, Thumbscrew, Weyfarers* and *The Yellow Crane.*

Some of these poems featured in *New Writing* published by Shoestring Press in 2001.

Thanks to East Midlands Arts for the award of a bursary in 2001.

CONTENTS

The Mountain:

BLACK SHEEP

(after a picture by Paula Rego)

Three bags full I ordered.
Got the number from the Yellow Pages –
'Black Sheep Enterprises'. He sounded
ever so nice on the phone.
When could he deliver? I said
the afternoon'd be fine.

Well I thought it was the devil:
black horns coiled like ammonites.
But there was something about him.
I stashed the wool away right quick,
let my red face cool.

And now my fingers work
a living fleece, one cloven foot
lost in the folds of my full skirt.

My little one is coming down the lane.
His days of nursery rhymes are numbered.

WEDDING DAY

The lilies are about to scream.
It will be clear, strident like the call
of white exotic birds who trail
green tails in still, still waters.

Their lips are curled
but florists' scissors snipped
their stamens out so all the guests
in pristine suits can brush
against them without risk.

The lilies are about to scream.
Their mouths yawn; tongueless
all the fire is gone. Permitted
lilies scented to no end. Like
yolkless eggs, tall candles
without wicks. Satin will shrivel
now the bells are mute.

THE POND

The heart had already gone out of our house
the summer you dug the pond. Day after
day, driving the old spade into clay,
bare-backed, your white limbs twitching
on the parched lawn, carving a womb.

I fought with dough in the dead kitchen:
brown bread for you, white for me.
We never ate together. You'd break pieces
from your loaf before it cooled – your usual
hurry to be somewhere else.

I wished the words the priest had made me say
unspoken, as I pressed the pill marked Thursday
from the packet. Standing beside the bed
I could not look out at the unfilled pond.

Empty of you, I pace through the rooms
on the upper floors. So many rooms
without a nursery air.

LAST JUDGEMENT, GROENINGE MUSEUM

You make a beeline for the Bosch,
which my guidebook describes
as a surrealist nightmare,
and begin your exaggerated scrutiny.

I leave you to stroll through other rooms,
stopping when something draws me:
a pasty-faced Madonna, time-darkened
saints resisting their temptations.

My route doesn't follow the logic
of the fold-out plan. I have to backtrack.
Still fixed on hell, you're careful
not to notice. I imagine

you've set yourself a target: one hundred
aimless tourists must pass by before
you raise your more informed eyes. Or,
better still – I'll prove impatient.

Bruges is beautiful; the sun's a bonus.
This modern gallery's purpose-built and light.
Things have been going well and so
you had to find your little patch of darkness.

BECAUSE SHE'S OUT

I heave myself out of your blue Capri
shuffle my weight from foot to foot, as you
insert your key into the door of the once
council-owned house. You can bring me here

this afternoon because she's out. I'm
curious I suppose, want to compare
the real thing with the picture that's
built up these past weeks in my head.

It's greyer inside than out and not
because it's Sunday minus the sun as usual.
A wall of stale smoke greets us. There's a
dinginess. Even the cushions are limp.

An unemptied ash tray – the kind that
people nick from pubs – sits tapping
distance from your bed. Somehow
I know that I'll never wake up there.

From room to room I follow as you
state the obvious. Kitchen's done in white –
not gleaming but the colour of cheap
T-shirts too often washed and wrung.

I think of her dusting the sad-looking ornaments;
you unpacking the kind of shopping which
I amuse myself condemning in other people's trolleys.
We kiss bloodlessly on your sofa.

SEEING STARS

Home, I unpack. My nightdress
smells of the country, of your house.
Restless, I walk outside, look at my sky –
it's a town sky. Half the stars are missing.

FENLAND BRIDE

I *Against the Gold*

I picture your heart as a map of the Fens:
neat compartments circumscribed
by straitened rivers, artificial cuts;

I haunt the fringes only. Sometimes
I drive and drive just to escape.
The roads are flanked by dykes

so deep an injured biker
lay out of view for days. Here
there is no room for manoeuvre.

As I head for Crowland, fields
gang up on me, uniform as graph paper;
even the flash of a tulip field neat

as soldiers on parade. I yearn for
the randomness of poppies shaking
their heads blood-wild against the gold.

II *Behind the Wheel*

Often – on my trips to anywhere – I'd be
slowed by tractors, their huge wheels

spinning out mile after arduous mile
as their exaggerated treads

spewed a detritus of straw,
dead confetti floating on the wake

of diesel fumes. I was always the one –
leading a train of frustrated motorists –

who was scared to pull out – even
when the road ahead was clear.

III   *Catch*

Killing time in the museum I read
that eels were used as currency: fifteen hundred eels
paid a Pinchbeck farmer's rent; four thousand
exchanged hands for building stone from Barnack.

And eels, with waterwolves, pickerels, turbot,
lamprey, perch were taken, live, to London
in hundred gallon butts. At every stopping place
they changed the writhing water.

In one case is a gleve – a cruel five-tined trident
used to spear eels and flip them into boats.
I imagine so much quicksilver stilled
and fading in a watery Fenland dawn.

Next there's an eel hive – a Christmas cracker shape
of wickerwork. I fix my gaze on the empty trap
and when, behind my back, the sun shifts,
a pair of glassy eyes stare back as captured light.

IV   *Tulip Parade*

Red tulips signify a love which burns
          after the decapitations heads by the million
with hearts so black to show how passion chars

are pinned to floats in decorative ways
Ferhad a Persian youth adored a maid
  paraded to the cheers of day-trippers
called Shirin. When she shunned him Ferhad fled
  coachloads clogging the arteries
into the desert, fallow as his hopes
  of this small town. Tamed blooms
his tears sprang to life as tulipan
  they will never throw off
named after tulbends Turks wind round their heads
  their pursed-lip primness
they slowly stretch exposing all their pain
  to let their petals yawn
contorting into acrobatic shapes
  in poses of wanton abandon
return to bulbs from which they'll rise again

V   *Gull*

Out of the corner of my eye
a gull spells freedom
in this sky of skies. Tricked
into acrobatics by vastness
it loops and gyres without
the safety net of the sea.

Used to the regal glide of ships
it fails to gauge the speed
of the white van. Falls jagged
from the air. I feel the day
contract. There's no telltale brown
of a young bird on its feathers –
it was old enough to know better.

It lies now on the tarmac.
The nearest waves are the brown,
static furrows of a ploughed field:
a place where crows rule.

VI   *The House on Horseshoe Road*

I've never had a sense of direction
to lose. Unless the sea's there

I can't say for certain which way
I'm facing. And even if I could

how would I know when a road
is upside down? This one must be –

all the luck's run out, even though
there's no tilt, no hint of a hill.

And when, in need of the drama
of cliffs, I drive to the coast,

the land sinks, abject, to the sea.
I head back across the Fens.

The sea has sucked the heart out.

VII   *Samphire*

Something thrives in this place:
its fleshy leaves – succulent, smooth
and moist with sea spray -
swell from the marsh.
A delicacy, I'm told.

Don't pull it up
before the longest day.
Go for those plants
that are washed by every tide.
Fresh water sucks the sap out.

I watch the sea recede. The moon
is late again. Night after night
I soak in a hot bath
praying for blood.

VIII   *Sour Milk*

I am not one for reading tea-leaves
but an owl ghosts across the surface
of my coffee on a day when you are out
again. No one has done the shopping.

By daylight the heart that is her face
will fade as ashes in a dying fire.
But at night, over the fens, on silent wings
she will rise, pale as ivory, from the ruins

she makes her home, the buff of her back
dusted with cinder grey. I crush the note
I'm left and push away the cup.
I do not have to drink.

MAGPIES

Of course it was a whale – that giant skeleton
suspended outside the faculty building.
But as soon as you said *What's that then?*
all the mammals I ever knew sensed my panic
and hurtled en masse out of the unstable ark of my head.

I made an abject stab at it. A mean smile rippled your face.
Don't you wish you'd done a degree in a real subject?
And I think of you categorising, scrutinising. Pinning
dead insects to a board. I can imagine by the age of five
your tide of logic would have drowned out Noah,

your imagination, the hapless raven sent out too early.
I know what ravens are and can identify their cousin crows
the magpies. Today, as I threw open your serviceable curtains
I saw one cawing in a nearby ash. I waited ages
but no others came. You wouldn't understand.

PAINTING BY NUMBERS

"......The disease which thus evolves these new and wonderful talents
and operations of the mind may be compared to an earthquake, which,
by convulsing the upper strata of our globe, throws upon the surface
precious and splendid fossils, the existence of which was unknown to
the proprietors of the soil in which they were buried."

Benjamin Rush

One thinks he does not have a heart.
They tore his soul out.
He says the cracking of his knees
is a telephone call. It's so
the devil down below
can know his whereabouts.

Grease crayon, body colours.
Toilet paper daubed with violet ink.
Sugar-bag, orange paper, scraps
of cloth. Necessity and ingenuity
are what they draw on.

One paints the souls of plants.
A once-watchmaker specialises
in watercolour miniatures.
Each tiny stroke
is a futile reordering.

They give their work strange titles:
Puff Poodle and Bulldog.
Skirt Metamorphoses. Horus
Dismembered. Retriever and Trained

Decoy Duck. The Photographically Verifiable
Interleaved Miraculous Images
Revealing a 15 Year Old Crime
in the Sole of the Victim's shoe.

Case number 40. Dementia praecox.
A businessman who flipped.
They give him paper and Indian ink
and he makes calendars, finds refuge
in chronology. As if the hooks
of neat calligraphy can stop
him falling.

Case number 308. No occupation.
On yellowing paper she writes
letters to a husband. Come. Sweetheart
come. She doesn't move her hand
to make new lines. The figures blur
and wave, so patterns spread like stains.
He never came.

He was a farmer, cultivated vines.
Now he draws trees. Their trunks
are soft, like tentacles. Fabulous fruit
is too symmetrically spaced. It hangs
from too symmetrical branches.
He names them: *Proud Earthly Tree*
with Little Bunches; *Cinderella's Slipper Tree.*
One has a raven on a branch that is
a trumpet. Case 116.

Hallucinatory insanity. He was
a photographer. Now he's case 121
and what he draws – with pencil, stumped
on thick cream paper – is like

an oblong print. *Toad Pond
at Full Moon.* Manic amphibians,
stilt-legs like walrus tusks
slither in moon lava. Grinning.

Schizophrenic paperhanger, case 402.
Mixed media on cardboard:
the gagged man pivots on crutches three times his size.
He swings his legs. The grey-green ground
will never catch him.

AFTER THE FALL

One arm covers her face as she
hugs herself in grief. He called her
the panther, raved about the fineness
of her muscles. Now, she feels the cold.

He has not guessed. Instead he alters
the contours of her belly, muttering.
He knows his eye is good. Perhaps
he blames the light – the lack of it.

This cold stuff seems to quicken as he works it.
She thinks of her Russian lover, the heat of him.
Next time, she knows, she won't be back.
The thing inside her kicks, firm as a rib.

He heard they fled to Italy, his Eve
unfinished. He watches the sun glance
off her navel, elbow, shoulder. He sees
the flaws and knows that it is good.

SHE WANTS

I don't mind when the beech tree nets
the sun as it sets, or when clouds choreograph
a tango of small rainbows on my floorboards.

But she wants all the honey for herself –
that languid light that graces late afternoons –
she wants to thrust three storeys in between

my house and what – for years – has been
my light. To pot the bright sun like
a billiard ball. In her (designer) pocket.

She plans to commandeer my sunsets –
to halt each pastel waltz so only she
can watch each shade shed partners

cleaving to others with chameleon ease.
It won't alleviate her brand of darkness.
She wants my not-quite-evening light

which lets the stair rail duplicate itself
in play-at-prison patterns on the wall.
She wants to make this real.

She wants my slice of night-light –
to raise her roof between
me and my moon. I will be left

blue-black and dangerous,
a silhouette, close
ally of the shadows…

KISSING GATE

When we were lovers, you talked often
of engaging. Apparently we didn't.
Not to your satisfaction, anyway:
I hadn't been to boarding school and you
weren't into rock bands.

One warm night in August
about a month before you left
we went walking, hand in hand beside a river –
passed through the kissing gates
along our path. I'd lead the way through one;
follow you through another.

I slide the thick black bolt across
my gate. It screeches out for oil.
The latch is skewed – will not lie flush.
It used to. Sometimes I take a hammer to it.

A kissing gate swings in its own enclosure.
Whoever named it understood that space
gives room to grow, helps separate things
click into place.

LETTER TO WILGEFORTIS

In a time of steeds she'd have placed
a peck of oats, as was the custom,
at the base of your statue.

She would have known your story
well. Instead, she chances on it:
a double-take at the plate of a bearded lady
in some musty hagiography.

You'd caught the fancy of a pagan king,
begged god to make you unattractive.
That heaven-sent moustache made
your suitor bristle. And your flesh father
had you promptly crucified.

Your other names – Uncumber, Liberata,
hint at your specialism: spouse disposal.
Well, husbands, anyway. She wonders if
you still oblige? If so, what should she offer
in this day and age? A can of petrol –
he could ride to the devil, even now.
Or will oats still suffice? You rig a race;
he legs it with some blonde.

I know she'll give
whatever it takes
to make that killing distance –
that started somehow, when she wasn't looking –
both physical and permanent.

FIRST KORMA

So *hot* you said – *you'll never finish it.*
I ate the lot and watched you
swilling down madras with beer.
You'd borrowed someone's cords
– yours were all worn – while I'd dressed down.
Some start! I nibbled on a spicy popadom. You bit
into a large peshwari naan
shaped like a heart.

OVERSPICED

The waiter at Islamabad
thinks I'm sweet as a jellabee.
You've been a shit
to me and I've been going there
with different guys.

He tries his luck in the cobbled lane
behind the restaurant. I hear my name
and turn. Saved by front-fastening dungarees
I run. He's pulled the button
off my sheepskin coat. It's 5 a.m.
You should have walked me home.

THE LAST CHAPATI

There's nothing left to mop up. On the edge
of the dish a spat-out clove, a wrinkled cardamom.
It started with a korma, that night
I let you order. Now I can make short work
of vindaloo. I tear the last chapati, pass
the smaller half to you.

DANGEROUS WATERS

The men I love
are as lighthouses.
They ignore the sea
when she throws up
her petticoats. Instead
they signal to each other
across oceans.
Always on the edge

strobing unsettled deeps,
their beams slice
through fog.
Upright as rockets
it seems as if the raging
froth and spume
will launch them
into another world.

JELLYFISH

While you are writing the letter
the one I will read over and over on Monday
in the dangerous cloakroom, I am safe
in the charmed circle of my black umbrella.

Insistent rain taps out a warning again
and again on the canopy. *It isn't right. It isn't right.*
But I don't listen and I will not think
about the sound of spring rain on the white marquee
four years before. It played a different tune.

I grip the handle – shaped like a walking stick
turned upside down. Like everything outside
this spoke-bound circle. It cannot steady me.
And I am envious of its frame of steel –
there's so much hurting to be done.

Bell-like I'm almost floating through this watery town.
I cannot look at my left hand. I know that soon
those things that brush the closest will be stung.

THE CEDAR TREE

You swung into my drive and left
the sun-roof gaping. And all that night
the reaching cedar made your car sing
shedding its strange confetti.

Storms took the tree. But blue-green needles
loiter, taunt – my lawn a January carpet.
Through the gap the road's more visible.
I could see further now if I were waving.

KISSING IN CUT-THROAT DENE

We shook off the always others
somewhere between Notrianni's

and the Jolly Sailor. The lane
wound for a mile past fields

pungent with oil-seed rape.
You tried to kiss me in the lay by

near the scout camp. But all the cars
kept tooting. We crossed the road

and screened by hawthorned mouth
of Cut-throat Dene I felt your tongue

still coldly sweet from ice-cream
and the hundreds and thousands

sprinkled on top swirled into
rainbows as I shut my eyes.

Later I inspect the only bruise
I've ever coveted. Leave the arm

of the turntable off so *Romeo*
by Mr Big plays on and on

and on. Until the nitty grit of sand
begins to scratch inside my baseball boots.

SPIN

Heading towards the Leas, I walk the cliff-top path.
It's April, and the windmill to the west
has caught the sun between its star-jump sails

as if to spin it into sudden summer. Or recreate
that fleece which hung in Colchis. It's a mirage
so absorbing, it seems, should I glance east

over grey waves, I'll see each gull turn albatross
and a squat boat streamline to an elegant Argo
with fifty frantic oarsmen pitching landward.

If I squint, the rock pipits which agitate the shoreline
are a chaos of pointing hands and nodding heads.
While the cormorant in the distance is a siren

seeking her sisters to deflect a theft.

THE WHORE FROM ORTACCIO

*The Carmelite Brotherhood reject Caravaggio's 'Death of the Virgin'
which they had commisioned for the high altar of the church of
Santa Maria della Scala*

She's stiff and swollen-bellied. Her bare feet
stick out from the wooden cot she's lying on.
And her dress – the kind that's worn by women
here in Trastevere, this place of narrow streets
filled with the poor – screams red
against her pallid flesh. Against all holiness.

'And wait' – it is the play of candle flame
on cheekbone which stirs dark memories
of a darker room – 'I know that face,'
says one who's looking on. He flushes then.

It turns out she's a whore from Ortaccio –
the artist's favourite, now the Queen of Heaven.

No angel choirs illuminate the bleakness.
Her open eyes stare past bare walls
to where a cross-beamed ceiling blocks out sky.

THE JAR

The jar was where I'd left it –
on a grimy windowledge
in the makeshift wooden garage.

I free it from the embrace
of cobwebs and discover
two Cabbage Whites dead
on foliage crisp as dried bayleaves.

More cruel than the swift pin
of an entomologist – wings, just freed
from a chrysalis stilled
in a coffin of glass.

The words you never said
flutter distractingly
luminous as the ghosts of butterflies
in a place dark with absence.

THE MOUNTAIN

I *Lighting the Butter Lamps*

At the great stupa of Bhodnath
we pause to light the lamps.
Our Chinese flasks are filled with melted butter.
We pour it into shallow pottery cups,

wait till the winds subside and light
each wick of twisted cotton, watch
the tiny flames dance in each other's eyes
and hearts. The gods look through them.

II *Puja (i)*

Oh – that was our Puja, she says
over Chardonnay, passing the photos round.
It's meant to make the gods give the OK
for expeditions – they all do it.
Some old monk chants and we bring offerings
– I gave some whisky and left-over chocolate –
and pass our climbing stuff through scented smoke –
juniper, if I remember right. Oh yeah – they're the...
prayer flags. At the end of it all we sang. She pauses
to spit out an olive stone. Then we all chucked *tsampa*
– that's a kind of flour – into the air and rubbed it
on our heads and in our cheeks so that we'd live
until our hair was white, supposedly! Look at him –
they believe this stuff those Sherpas. He's the one
we lost. Just one more set, I promise! Then we'll eat.

III *Lung-ta*

A wind horse shakes his mane
and the air is thick with mantras,
susurrations.

Surefooted he will surge
through storm clouds
hoof-prints precise

as heartbeats of the pure.
Unloosed by tainted minds
his kin will weave

aimless as snowflakes
over the bleached bones
of the lost.

IV *Puja (ii)*

At the heart of the lapso we build a mound
of stones. A monk is brought from Pangboche.
I offer bread and a little barley,
pray that the gods will bless our expedition.
My heart is pure enough but I can sense
the woman's mind is clouded with the need
to prove herself. *Chana* we call it – this fear
of being beaten. Such strong desires
pollute our undertaking and the gods
will turn their backs, leave us to storm,
to serac and crevasse. Or avalanche.
She sneaks a prayer flag as a souvenir.
I pass my ice axe through the incense twice.

V   *The Cry of the Gorak*

It will rain blood if you cry
so much. It will veil his eyes
and the way to a rebirth will be a blur.
They say this to me at his funeral.

When the sahibs came, I think, it was then
he couldn't see straight. *The mountain's angry*
I told him – *at what they bring and what*
they leave behind. But he went anyway.
And when the gorak swept across our field
I knew their boldness made the mountain shudder
and caught him in the spindrift.

The wind carried my keening,
to where his body lay. His soul clung
to the broken shell, unsettled by my cries.
When silence came, I felt him slip
from me. And the gorak bore his soul away.

The harsh *kraak-kraak* rings in my ears
as fire rises with the setting sun.
The sky is turning red.

VI   *Chukpö Lare*
(The Sherpa burial ground on Mount Everest)

We mould his ashes into a votive tablet,
and place this *tsa-war* inside a small shrine
we've built of stones. It does not bear his name.

He lay all night on the Lhotse face
prey to malevolent spirits. We waited for a calm
and brought him here, to Chukpö Lare.

33

The lama's scarlet robe leapt with the fire
in which his body burned. We watched the smoke disperse
breathed in the scent of Juniper. He will lose himself

in death, as in that whiteout when he fell,
when flake on unmatched flake lost its uniqueness
compacted into ice.

VII   *The Sherpa's Lament*

Now she has spoken
our mountain, she the goddess
mother of the world.

Forehead in the sky
the wrath of Sagarmatha
is cloaked in storm clouds.

Our ancestor's fled
from terror in the lowlands.
Safe in her shadow

we did not keep faith,
failed to bar intruders from
her sanctuary.

See how they trample
her limbs. Litter and profane
her sacred slopes.

Souls of those she takes
wander, helpless as prayer-flags
in a godless world.

VIII *Letting Go*

High on Dhaulāgiri the sickness
strikes. His footfalls slur behind
my own neat prints. Back in our tent

I hold him as his breath rasps out
jagged as flag cloud, and the grip
of the mountain closes.

I clip our lucky rope to his harness
– the link that never frayed on Aconcagua,
Denali, Kosciusko. Drag him stiff limbed

across the ice to where it splits.
As I lower him into that grim rictus,
I close my eyes but I can feel

the thing that bound us
slipping through
my hands.

AUGURY

The first time my ear met your loud heart
I could not look up. I was like an augur
out of practice, who, with desire and dread
waits for the sudden sweep of some great wings.

Bdoom, bdoom, bdoom. Seconds as far
apart as the big stars. And later, when
we reminisced in sheets whose creases
left no room for doubt, you told me
you'd worried how I'd read those beats…

And it's your honesty, disarming, sudden,
like the flight of birds, which makes
the clouds fly and the lightning fork.

EDGES

Awkward, all angles
of elbows and briefcase,
suited and unfamiliar
you arrive.

I knew you wouldn't
kiss me. Still I'm dampened
slightly breathless
from that hasty zig-zag across the footbridge
fraught with couples and puddles.

Through dinner and through a play
we sit stiffly, parallel as
the red pinstripes on your shirt.

Later, quilted, in darkness,
we will meet and melt as ice floes
while the strangeness gives an edge.

AFTER THE FLICKS

Only your lips
could meet me anywhere
in the back of your Dad's Fiat
parked part way down a dirt track
after the Saturday flicks.

That night of the half-and-half moon
I was brought up sharp
by the probe of a stranger's headlights
and something luminous
snagged in the hawthorn.

WALKING TO SCHOONHOVEN

The methodical tick of a bicycle chain
warns my ear of what is behind, but I
concentrate on the road ahead – a goat or two
cropping grass beside high-gabled houses,

a heron moving station with leisurely
sweeps of his huge grey wings. Unhurried,
I take my cue from them. After all
there are hours to kill before evening

when I'll sit again, while you attend
another meeting. And your new wife finds
important things to do – as if to say
my husband – he invited you.

At Hoek van Holland, where I waited yesterday
for the train, October poplars were scrawny.
In my window seat I could smell stale beer
from empty bottles in the nearby bin.

Today at the silverhuys I'm told silver's not antique
until a century's past. Till then it's second hand.
I hope friendship's merit is relative – takes
less time to appreciate. Somehow I doubt it.

On my way back, I look out for the tree
whose bare branches laden with ripe golden pears
can be seen clearly now the screen of leaves has dropped.
It's like a picture on a Christmas card. Or a parable.

Tomorrow, en route to a prior engagement, you'll drive me
to the station. After our polite goodbyes you'll leave.
Too early for the boat-train, I'll find a locker for my bags
and fumble with the unfamiliar small change.

SKETCH

On Sunday afternoons when I was drawing
you'd fetch your stanley knife and steal my pencils,
thumb-turn each deftly, shave till it was sharp.

When you had done I'd pick each one and sniff
its cleaned wood smoothed and fluted like a lily.
The coloured stamens made my paper bloom.

THE BRIDGE

The bridge is seventy this year. As a small boy
you stood on the bank at the Gateshead side –
were sure the bits begun at either end
would fail to meet. You tell me this
as we sit in a quayside cafe over toast.
We giggle as you scrape another butter wrapper clean
when one would do – knowing what Mum would say.
The café is right underneath the bridge.

You've pointed out the office where you worked
in '51 – *before I met your mother*. It's all
glass and flashness now, but nostalgia
doesn't tarnish in your case. You are as thrilled
by the new as you are to show me the armada anchor
pinned to the wall near the tucked-away almshouses
or chance upon the corner where you parked your Riley.

Somewhere behind you is another bridge
which spans a river very far from here. You were
so nearly a statistic – they say each sleeper
claimed at least one life.
                              Squinting into the sun
we head back to the car park, curb the urge
to spit at any Nissans (half in jest).
As I glance across the tarmac to the river,
an ugly vessel trails a wake of gold.

COUNTING

How I longed for Tristram's grackle
blue-footed boobies, roseate starlings.
A glimpse would do. And Frances would
be hopping – her lucky spoonbill well and truly
ousted! But she'd never wear it.
So I stayed indigenous – but sort of lied about
the red-backed shrike. It was there, honestly –
twenty pairs of frenzied binoculars
focused on its head. But all I got was tree.

I thought about borrowing
the giant frigate bird that Kevin
(our Y.O.C leader) claimed he sighted
off the north east coast. But I stuck
with the Slavonian grebes
that I'd really seen bobbing one winter
in the surf off Cullercoats.

We struck tick after frantic tick
by the lists in our bird spotter's field charts,
gold kestrels hovering in our lapels.
Longed for exotic visitors –
ornithological one-upmanship.
How could we know in thirty years
house sparrows would be in decline
or that it would be something
in summer just to hear
a song thrush in your garden.

GOOD ENOUGH TO EAT

I hear the jaunty click
of a wren in conifer
by clovered verges

green-starred with gorse
and the whir and stir
of an unseen bird

in the birch-fleece.
I skirt a field
rusty with sorrel

wavy with torn
windsocks of cottongrass,
eyed by wild raspberries.

The hillsides are
pastel with heather
as I pick my way over

paths acrawl with toads
small as nut clusters
the colour of chocolate.

SHARKS

She hitches up her skirt for the zoom lens
to home in on the scar. I feel a livid echo

in my chest. Each tooth mark on her thigh's
a deep, red bead – much like the necklace

that you never bought, but which appears
somewhere about my heart in sleep

and hardens there like tyre tracks in mud.
She wears it well. *I have a new respect*

for sharks. Nods at the surfboard. *No –*
it hasn't put me off. I must not flinch

each time your silver car, its wide grill grinning
swims out from shallows in this too small town.

NOT A HAIR ON MY HEAD

I focus on a muted pillar-box marooned
by building work; anaemic geraniums;

a trail of booted glass and then the gape
of a morning-after phone booth.

There isn't any anger left. OK, I am aware
that I'll soon be walking past your street –

the unfamiliar end. Years and short-sightedness
conspire to make me squint. *Yes it's the one.*

I look ahead and not away but as I stop to cross
I'm fingering my hair – I wear it down now –

a sign of agitation. Then the green man flashes
and I think *there's not a hair left on my head
that you have touched.*

SEEING RED

In spite of their warnings, I was losing myself
there are huge red poppies in the rectory garden
I didn't realise – they said beware of men who are
tall, so tall, they are racing the delphiniums to the sky
so exacting – but I thought yes I can cope
with scarlet frills – which shameless have burst the tight buds
I am equal to this and I so wanted
like creased gifts of scandalous lingerie
to be the thing he wanted me to be
to flounce with the physicality of gypsies
oblivious to the damage somewhere inside
and the in-your-eye bravado
which ate away slowly, but with the potency
of a Whistler nocturne – the sort
which eases with the passing of many moons
that Ruskin was afraid of

JONATHAN

Your youngest brother will miss school on Monday.
He'll be screened at the haemotology clinic
to see if his bone marrow matches yours.

Your Mum's floral notepaper, her ordinary script
are at odds with the stark news:
this week what was suspected was confirmed.

At sixteen you threw off school for college
and the uniform you'd complemented with a nose stud.
I'd turned a blind eye while the hole was raw.

I picture the slantwise scrawl of your essays
– grade A, but indecipherable, at times,
as the squiggles on a heart monitor. Recall that day

you shaved your head. When I last saw you
at the station you tugged up a fading T-shirt
to shock me with your newly pierced navel.

Grey cells of cloud invade a clear stretch
of sky as I wander back from posting
the book I hope will make you laugh.

They had looked at me oddly in Smith's
as I scanned each page anxious to ascertain
what the heroine's father died of.

Angina, in his sixties. At university your final year.
I bite my lip, try for another adjective.
And focus on the narrowing patch of blue.

HOT LOVE

In '72 he was my main man. My ear glued
to a cheap transistor as the double decker lurched
through glitterless suburbs to the comprehensive.

I'd carve his name in every desk I sat in –
a point of honour. Head full of lyrics to add mystery
to Mrs Rapley's slides of igneous rocks.

A tube of eye-shadow from Woolworths
purple – his favourite colour (so it said in *Jackie*)
for the night he jumped from a star at City Hall

and older girls threw knickers on the stage. I thought
I might faint as I waved my scarf and screamed
with less flat-chested children of the revolution.

I stuck with him through the vodka and the pills.
Bought *Popswap*, *Music Star* – to trade the toothy Osmonds
the Jackson 5 or David Cassidy for his now rarer face.

He left me dreaming of that local boy who sprayed
MARC BOLAN LIVES on a gable end and then ran off
to say goodbye, see for himself the white swan made of flowers.

REVENGE TRAGEDY

There wasn't a real murder – or any blood
for that matter. But on my left wrist
there's still the faint pink ghost
of a carpet burn from the Somalian rug –
the one that's in your living room.

Those times when I took things lying down
haunt me like clichés in a bad romance.
I never got you back – that's the tragedy of it.

LAST WORD

You won't remember me, the humble artisan.
I've come a long way since… well, I'll not speak of *that*.
I paint the tombs of great ones, like yourself. So, after all
this time, we meet again. Except you're in a box – a pretty
grand one, granted, all overlaid with gold.
Gearing yourself up for the afterlife.

Everything's finished, except these here paintings.
They've left me to it. Reliable I am, see? Never been known
to get it wrong. It's what I paint that counts. OK,
you've been embalmed. No unguents spared – even
some extra stored in alabaster jars. And yards of linen
holding you together. But you'll rot, we all do.

That's where I come in. Your spirit'll live in this.
That's why we have to paint in everything. It wouldn't do
to be without your bits – not with eternity just round the corner.
Where all the crops are taller, cattle fatter,
where silver fish are begging to be caught
and beer and wine flow like the Nile in flood.

Oh dear, I've just dropped that deep blue bowl –
with lotus flowers unfolding to the dawn! And now
I'll move this big canopic chest so that it rests
right underneath my work. And then the priest who checks
and seals the door will fail to notice that
you will go legless to the Field of Reeds.